# AUGUST LIGHT

Other books by the author:

# *August Light*

PETE MORGAN

**ARc**
PUBLICATIONS
2005

Published by Arc Publications
Nanholme Mill, Shaw Wood Road
Todmorden OL14 6DA, UK

Copyright © Pete Morgan 2005
Design by Tony Ward
Printed by Antony Rowe Ltd
Eastbourne, E. Sussex, UK

ISBN 1 904614 23 X

Acknowledgements are due to the editors of the following publications where many of these poems first appeared: *Dream Catcher, Ixion, The Haiku Quarterly, Lines Review, Poetry Australia, Poetry Review, Poetry Wales, New Statesman, New Welsh Review, The Slab, The Scotsman* and *Poetry Please!* (BBC Radio 4). 'From 'I': to 'I'' was written to celebrate the 82nd birthday of Sir Stephen Spender and first appeared in *A Garland for Stephen Spender* (The Tragara Press, Edinburgh. Editor: Barry Humphries). 'Returns of the Day' was commissioned by the National Arts Collection Fund and first appeared in *The Arts Quarterly*. The picture which the poem celebrates is 'Many Happy Returns of the Day' (William Powell Frith, 1818-1909), purchased by The Mercer Art Gallery, Harrogate, in 1951 with assistance from the NACF. York City Art Gallery purchased an earlier study of the same picture with a contribution from the National Arts Collection Fund in 1991. 'Get thee Glass Eyes' was commissioned by The Globe Playhouse Trust and first appeared in *Poems for Shakespeare 10* (editor Charles Osborne). Poems contained in Section II result from a writer-in-residence post at Whittingham Psychiatric Hospital, Preston. This post was completed under the auspices of Arts Council England in conjunction with Preston Health Authority. The Whittingham poems first appeared in *Away...*, a limited edition pamphlet from Driftwood Publications, Liverpool. (2003).

Cover: *August Light* (silkscreen print)
© Michael Carlo, 1983

The Publishers acknowledge financial
assistance from ACE Yorkshire

**Editor for UK / Ireland: Jo Shapcott**

*To G.B.*
*M.D., M.Chir., F.R.C.S.*

*without whom*

# Contents

**I**

First Off / 13
Fish / 14
God Picks Winkles / 15
Seal / 16
Flurry / 17
A Midnight Craft / 18
Bats / 20
NP94B 1721 / 21
Badgers / 22
Good Orts / 23
Finds / 24
In August Light / 28
*First On* / 29
In Tens / 30

**II**

Cleaners / 35
David in the Daffodils / 36
Walter's Ramble / 37
Amy's Tale / 38
Amy's Bedside Photograph / 39
Michael on the Make / 40
Chance Encounter / 41
Night Sweats / 42
Bedtime Story / 43
Taking Leave / 44

**III**

Late Fire / 47
A Passionate Adventure / 48
Safe Lupins / 50
The Bullfinch & the Buffalo / 52
*In Absentia* / 53
June 3 / 54
Sir Pig / 55
No Metamorphoses / 59
No Moon, no Star / 60
Mirror, *Mirror* / 62
'*Warum, Warum...*' / 64
The Man who wrote '*Deutschland*' / 66


**IV**

Crab Apple / 69
"Get thee Glass Eyes..." / 70
Written on a Green Screen / 72
From 'I' To 'I' / 73
'Returns of the Day' / 74
Afterthought / 75


Biographical Note / 77

It was not that he became a lesser poet
  neither did he
  consciously stop writing.
Seven years in that same city
  and he high-tailed out
for anywhere. For eighteen months he kept
the back door open; let the town house as a bond
  in case the country palled.

The country was his death. It did not pall.
  A hundred miles
  from the nearest poet,
friend, and therefore critic, he found
  a new freedom,
a freedom to write what he wanted when
he wanted. A freedom not to have to write,
  to keep his poems in his head.

                    from *The Poet's Deaths* (1977)

I

# First Off

As starting point an April gull
kicks from pantile into sky –

unfolding into cruciform,
breaking into swoop and sinew,

tucking everything but his beak
into that bundled appetite
of beady eye, of gullet straining.

He trails his aim along the tideline,
swings his sight across the scaur,
hauls his claw from fear to flurry –

kicks from solace into sun.

# Fish

The fish we haul from dark to light
smack and flicker at the sun –
angry with their own decision,
raging at their muscle's failure
tapering to helplessness.

They snap off from the line like fruit –
not the rip of hook through flesh,
more the sound of something plucked
from earth's hold or the grip of sap.

They thump against the bottom board –
their colours bruising into grey,
their fury banging in the brain
but weakening with every pulse
like old men tired of trying.

# God Picks Winkles

Yesterday through rock and wrack
Someone in God's likeness stepped
Between the tideline and the sea
And bent to judgement, made his choice
From rock pools where his image quivered.

Between the cold yawn of his jaws
God's likeness slid his fingers in
And pulled his eye-teeth from his head –
Each one inch gem, each ridge of shell
Cleated to the earth's foundation.

What a wind it was which spun
Each lick of spittle from each root
And what a fearful hand it was
Which slid beneath the bucket's rim
Each small extraction, one by one.

Last night in his feather bed
God's likeness lay with sibilance
Rising toward him in his heaven,
Heard the poppled pleas for mercy
Louder than his stomach's churning.

Today God's likeness woke and found
His own teeth, pulled and chattering,
Had climbed from water into air
And gathered at the bucket's rim –
Their small prayers answered.

What a certain hand it was
Which swung the bucket to the shore
And poured the teeth back to the head –
And what a knowing eye it was
Which watched God's grin begin to broaden.

# Seal

Late night, between the fishing boats
a sudden sound, *'Man Overboard!'*? –
    and then it eases, just the lull
of tugging at the moorings, just
the slap slap of the sea's calm rise:
    but then it starts again, a fair
way off but far more alien. –
Quick breakers shake the moon, the stars.

First light at dawn: the agony
of rips in net, where last night's catch
    already hung and drawn hangs hard
as wet rope: dead weight, broken too
the heart, the haul; the stink of fish
    from dock to dump in deeper seas.
Out of sight if not out of mind
the flip flop slip of fish on fish.

This sea-rat slaughterer is known:
by day she brags her pride to dip
    and dive, without a flick, without
a ripple; unafraid in seas
decreed *'Dangerous for Bathers'*.
    By night she turns to lifter, dip
who filches fish from nets and fills
the morning tide with fillets, fins.

On land she struggles in her skin
to shuffle sand and leave a trail
    of each fin digging, furrowing
and take her time to reach a place
where she can shelter, unafraid.
    And here it ends: shotgun, cudgel,
take revenge in blood, in bruising
into an ugly nudge of sea.

# Flurry

Even the gulls were bitter mourners,
their stark cries were of desolation.
Jolted from the night to day
they rose from rock
and soared to light.

Something had come to some bleak ending,
something not trivial but huge,
something made significant.

And they rose to find out what it was;
could not find out what it wasn't,
could not find out what it had been,
could not discover what it might become.

But something had put a flurry in them;
something had stirred a wing to strike,
something had risen and sunk back.

And they wheeled once, twice
and again they landed,
settled back to where they had been,
folded their white wings, each to each
and went on being gulls again.

## A Midnight Craft

*for Seamus Heaney*

**Hook**
Late last night I went to catch a fish
and found the same fish took the hook.

The first hook I had cast had ripped the lip.
I knew that lip. I knew that ooze of blood

where blood had wept in water to the gill.
I saw that gill again. I saw that cut

where I *had had* to cut to set him free
and I felt free when I first felt the flick

of fish against the wrist, the flick of fin
against each thumb. That thrum of fin let shift

all hint of blame. His shift was in one whip
of rippled water. My whip hooked the moon

down from the moon in heaven to the pool
where one bright pool of white light glittered. *Fish.*


**Line**
In the moon's whorl where I cast the line
a line of silver ripples rose

to patter like rose petal in the wind.
From that wise wind I tried to wind a word

to catch the right word once but never twice
for twice might crack the mirror of the moon

reflecting moon or shattered star. But that
was that! The fingers flickered at the nip

but bided time for that quick nip to hold.
I felt that hold. I felt the barb bite through

and through the wristy winding of the reel
I wound the reel. I played the canny game

but found no game in him; no heft, no haul.
I found the same haul hooked fast on the line.


  **Sinker**
In my hand I felt the writhe of weight
but there was no lead weight to sink

the barb and sink the bait. The hook was lost
and I was lost. I fought the snood to snap –

it would not snap: I fought the pocket knife
to knife the line: I fought the blade with tooth.

The tooth bit through the half an inch of air
to cleave the air. I felt the quick gash grip

to grip the lip and tug the gullet. Now
I felt the hook and now, and now, the tease

that I *had had* to tease to win that prize.
I was that prize. I was that dive to deep

where through the deep I dithered god's good eye
between the hook's eye, line and lead-shot weight.

# Bats

Nothing in heaven moves like that –
not moth, not hawk, not shooting star.

Here is the anti-geometric. The thumb-
screw, blind turn, leading nowhere.

Here is the ugliness of flight,
the bogey bearaway from Hell.

Here is the flightpath gone electric
in fizzing volts of energy –

not patternless but needle perfect,
tacking the several stars together.

I look for kindle, find a purity
of white which draws me to one corner where
there is one fallen pigeon on the stone.

Each feather shifts in air, one reach of wing
is beating out a slower rhythm than
the batter she would hammer at the wind.

There is no wound. She lies immaculate
with one pink claw outreaching, one claw held
against the fur and feather of the breast.

I pick her up and find her dead weight more
than those slim inches from the tip to tail.
All I can do is keep her from the rot.

I snap the leg to crack the ring away
and feel that brutal breakage shudder through
the fingers and the shoulder to the gut.

I keep her from the wind and from the worm
and take her where I was to take the wood
to leap the chimney of the burner. There

she slips with grace and sizzles up to huff
her instant puff of smoke against the blue
now cleansed and calmed by yesterday's dull storm.

# Badgers

In the middle of the road a badger stoops
licking the white no-overtaking line.
It must be ants or dew, I think,
perhaps the blood of some past accident.

He doesn't shift but lifts his head –
looks directly at the car. His eyes reflect
the headlights on full beam
and shine as white as opal glass.

I blow the horn. No fear in him.
He stays, returns to licking at the line.
I slip to first, inch forward then he shifts
and starts his lollop following the road

but not just him: five of them, all sizes
leap from the hedgerow and the verge.
They do not give the slip back to the sett
but like keen schoolboys following the ball

lock on the white line of the road
where headlights blaze a tunnel in the trees.
Hooped shirts heaving, white shorts mucked
the whole run is formation of a scrum –

the hooker, two props on his left and right,
the two wing forwards holding back but ready.
The game goes on too long. I must be home.
I swing into a lay-by, light the woods.

They're off! Crashing through bracken into dark
but one of them halts, turns his head
and shows again his bright eyes burn –
a slap on the back at the final whistle.

# Good Orts

The working worm, the wind, the rain
unearth the reawakening
in broken blinks of porcelain –
the delft, the crackleware, the spode;
in gobs of glass, in shives of chine –
the rat, the weasel, and the ox.

To shift the earth with iron assists
the wrench of root, the slow upheave
which turns today from yesterday –
the crack of crockery, the clink
of metal against metal's blight –
'GEORGIVS V DEI GRA:BRIT:'

Reverse: Britannia, verdigris –
the shield worn thin by years of spin
against the grindings of a ground
which rises like a rising tide
of snicks and snippets, sharp shiveens
of some lost sorrow swallowing

the light of rediscovery.
The pieces never fit, no chip
of china fits the next dull crock
of earthenware returned to earth.
No metal lets the secret free
but *they* return, reflected in

the ownership of shattered finds –
the cup, the candlestick, the urn,
the lock, the key, the broken bell
which clangs one off-key on the earth
cluttered with smithers of good orts
to wink their thousand eyes at rain.

# Finds

### 1. Crack Derby     c. 1897
She, whoever she was, slipped her finger
through the handle of bone china, acted
as though she'd done it all her life and knew
precisely how to raise her little pinkie
and watch it bend correctly when the cup
was raised above the level of her guest's.
It seemed important, at the time, the act
of sipping tea with elegance.

She sipped, and tried to talk, but always seemed
to chink the cup against the saucer. Now
she knew that wasn't how it should be done
but tried her level best to get it right.
Her man was no great shakes. He sometimes came
when she had thought he would be on the field.
But he, whoever he was, *'Ad a bash*
*at suppin' owta china.'* Once.

### 2. Brass Buckles, Buttons     c. 1918
A single turn of earth beside the wall
cut to the root of something best forgot –
or so the lad who laid the fire thought
when he turned out his tunic in a heap
and doused with paraffin. He did not stay
to watch the fire flourish. As for smoke
he knew that he had sniffed enough of that
to last what little he had left.

There was some more to burn beside the stuff
he'd taken from his pockets. He ran in
and stripped off on the landing, threw it down
to where his mother waited at the door.
She took it out but failed to understand
why he had lost all pride in what he'd worn.
She folded khaki neatly, with regret –
but saw him mouthing her, *'Get on!'*

### 3. Lead Shepherd     c. 1939

Up to the shanks in soil the shepherd sinks
backwards, looking up to rain, and praying
for a lung less leaden, heart less heavy.
The moustache grizzles, the right hand clutches
tight to the hem of the embroidered smock
as he knee-bends the contralto's curtsey –
the eyes far-distant, the smile uncertain.
He trusts his trade will be made known

by the dimpled hat, the dinted gaiter
but always he dreams of his lost left arm
slung on a hook in the doll's house kitchen –
of the old dog sunk in the water butt,
the shepherd's crook tight in the toothless jaw.
The sheep mistake the shepherd's woolly mind
and never ever read him right. All sense
is lost in his blind eye, deaf ear.

### 4. Tin Sheep     c. 1939

A yard away, to scale, is not a mile –
more like a hundred yards or so, a field
with no stone wall across the land to halt
the sheep returning homeward to the fold.
The shepherd cannot see the sheep, not know
his distance from the ewe is no great shakes
for earth has shaken. What was once a moor
is now a range of tumps and tors

no sheep will bother clambering unless
there is no reason for the climb. Today
the sheep continues being sheep, she keeps
her head down to the ground where grass once grew
but nuzzles nothing. Nothing worries her,
not passing time, the shadows creeping in.
Across her peaks and pikes have crept for years.
The shepherd starts to count; *'Yahn, Tarn...'*

### 5. Eley-Kynoch 12     c. 1946

There is no beauty in this trophy now.
All that is left, the metal of the base
which names the makers, indicates the bore,
and that's been fired, the hammer's struck the point
and something's either been hit or been missed.
Though hit's more likely with a twelve bore spread
which peppers air and cuts the target down
to some deft certainty of death.

Nothing can tell quite what the target was
or who it was who took the butt-end up
then touched the trigger and was comforted
by something either dying or quite dead.
But what was certain was he owned a gun
and that possession brings the man again
to throw his shadow on the earth he owned,
to raise the barrel and take aim.

### 6. Scissors     c. 1953

It wasn't just that light was fading. No,
she knew that other things beside her sight
were slipping but she didn't dare to think
what made her keep some things to hand, forget
and come downstairs to breakfast, comb still held:
or go out in her pinny to the shop.
She kept that to herself all Friday, kept
the good stitch good as ever was.

Come Saturday her grandson had to cut
a photograph of Lofthouse from the *Chron.*
He asked for scissors. When she looked she found
no scissors in the basket so he ripped
the picture from the paper. Ten years on
he found the scissors in the garden where
she'd laid them closed beneath the tree, tight shut –
the two blades rusted tight by rain.

## 7. Sylvo    c. 1957

Between the mould of laurel and the shield
the metal of the medal's clogged with lime.
Within a loop of silver rope, a boy,
astride an upright bicycle stands still:
stock still, beneath an overhang of cloud.
Between each hub and rim each spoke is choked
with Sylvo; that full promise of a prize
once gloried in and glorified.

Between the good intention and the act
came second thoughts. The drip of dribble dimmed
the silver key into a fog and dulled
the shimmer of the cross-bar and the boy.
A burnish on the denim – one wild whoop
and spinning the medallion on the palm
against the light the shadow shifts the knee –
the white tape whips across the wheel.

## In August Light

there is that changeability;
that subtle shift from summer
into turning, and all of it
in sudden slips of wind,
or else the scurry of a cloud.

In time it took to turn a page
or else to open up a gate
we pace the barrier between
a passing joy, a ray of hope
or else a memory of sorrow.

In August light there is no need
to hunt the promise of fair weather.
In just a day it comes to us –
the labour of the harvest shows
there is no longer summer left to kill.

## First On

*First On* came through mist to mist
his huge bulk looming colourless,
stepping through from grey to grey –
even his voice a low foreboding.

*First On* came wan and shadowless –
his even pace not telling tales
of that abundance at his belt,
the soft pelts merging into dew.

Only his absence kept repeating,
stepping through from fret to fret,
something not quite right, the rifle
protruding from the silhouette.

## In Tens

When I was ten my father won a pig –
A half a pig, to be exact, not whole.
He hung it high and head down in the shed
So in the lamplight through the open door
It shone as plump and perfect as a pig.
I never asked him what he won it for.
He told me how it must be hung to drain
The black blood in the bucket at the neck,
How after draining it would take good salt
To keep it from the rot, last least a year.

That pig had bled already, swear I heard
Just ten drops in the bucket's echoing.
My father went back in the house. I stayed
And found the perfect lash upon the eye
Which looked to me like sleeping, not like death.
And on the gob, tight shut, I swear a grin
Was shifting toward me. I heard laughter ring
And slammed the door tight shut and ran back in
To where my mother, rocking in her chair,
Held to her breast her baby. He was pig!

I did not speak to father any more
About his fine reward, his prize of pig.
Just ten days after winning he was gone.
My mother came to break the news to me
And found me sitting upright in the bed
And telling her that I already knew.
I did not tell her how I had foreseen
My father hanging head down in the shed,
His throat a gash of crimson and each eye
Tight shut like I once saw him in his sleep.

Just ten days after burial my mam
Demanded how we had to cut the pig
Down from his secret gallows in the shed

And salt the skin so he would keep. It took
A ladder to reach up to cut the rope,
A barrow to parade him to the house.
I lay him in the kitchen by the fire
And started what was truly an assault.
In no way could you call it a massage.
It wasn't just ten minutes. Ten times that!

There was some exorcism in the act
Of hammering the flesh out with the hand
As that pig wobbled to each blow then lay
As though he needed more salt in each wound.
His skin was rough; each bristle seemed to cut
A scar between the fingers of each hand.
I hoped it was the acid in the salt
And not some unknown chemistry to act
To resurrect the living from the grave.
We cut him into ten fine joints of pork.

That night as I lay wide awake in bed
I had to hold each hand out from the sheet
For each was singing with a sting of pain
Which had me weeping. Salt cut in the wound.
But what I know now is that hurt, that pain
Was not to do with pig but was the guilt
Of losing someone I had never known
And never got to know. What I now know
Is how we tidy life up in the mind.
Nothing is ever quite as neat as tens.

II

# Cleaners

The jokers rule the ward.
Each day their false authority
demands attention. They shift
each pawn around the board
into the path of king or castle
and laugh it off, as though
each shift from space to space
obeys all rules of cleanliness
and comfort. Each bed is made,
tight-fitting as a plaster cast,
each bed-side cabinet re-dusted,
each pillow pouffed to some perfection
of creaselessness and chastity.

*'No soul may rest on this bed until bed'.*
From ward to ward the bad jokes shift
leaving behind a polished silence
with no hands clapping, no encore –
and the whole ward wiped and empty.

# David in the Daffodils

Good Friday and the cricket pitch as sodden
and rippled as an English lake in winter
and David attempts his derring-do step
across the mown grass, barren as Auschwitz.

Out there, among the bowing and the bending,
he sings his praise for goldenness and good
but in his manic dance he tramples hope
back to the earth which was to be his Zion.

On his return he weeps a private pain:
not at the cold but at the cripple in him
who wreaked such ruin where he went to praise
and stamped each star with his slow staggering.

# Walter's Ramble

His is the language of distorted sense:
the single phrase repeated and repeated
until, before the end, intention gathers
the final words into a galloped gab
of something made from puzzlement to prize.

And prize is prized. With an uncertain pride
words gathered are repeated and repeated
until, before the end, some interruption
might halt the thought, might twist the hidden meaning
back to the brain which shuffled word from word.

A question asked, no sense begins again:
the single syllable repeated and repeated
until, before the end, each word assessed
and proven is tumbled to the next –
from syllable to word, from word to phrase –
from phrase to sentence into some sense made.

And there's the pride which leads to repetition
like holding up the cut glass to the light.

## Amy's Tale

It came as a surprise at first
to find myself silently escorted
into a mix of corridors, big rooms
where strangers leaned against white walls,
some of them sobbing, clutching clothes,
some of them talking to themselves.

But then at night the shouting started
from iron beds into what darkness
was allowed, all of it sickened by the safety light,
thin curtains. And then the crying started in me,
rose to the ceiling; wet the pillow.
The nurse's torchlight – *'Cut that out!'*

But soon I grew quite used to it.
Used to no knives, no forks, all spoons –
used to not wearing what I wanted,
used to the door being loudly bolted,
used to my man no longer calling –
and all to do with that easy thing –
the man I loved, the love I gave,
and the child he gave to me, not wanted.

# Amy's Bedside Photo

He crouches in the on-your-marks,
the knees already tensed and bending,
each finger and each thumb tip
touching earth,
each toe tip straining
through the sandal's leather.

The back's well humped,
the head's well down
and no eye turns to fix the camera.

In the distance the smiling figure,
out of focus, is ready to drop
the nurse's hankie.

There is no opposition in the race:
no friend, no stranger,
no identifiable rival.

And on the back, in faded pencil,
the name's confusion, the years preciseness –
*'Arthur now Andrew: aged six, 1948'.*

# Michael on the Make

Michael is good. He doesn't smoke.
But daily he collects his ration –
keeps it a week or so maybe,
mounts it in a plastic case
and shuffles down the corridor
in his old grey suit, bow tie
and polished slippers.

Outside the chill of the Smokers' Room –
the windows open always,
the ashtrays all in overflow,
high ceilings tainted nicotine –
a quick scrum gathers, reads his price
scrawled in biro inside the pack.

This tout never mouths a word.
There is no bargaining, no barter.
He is dumb to those who press or plead.
Quick as a light he gets his price.
In the passageways of poverty
the sale of the cig. is his economy.

# Chance Encounter

There comes that moment when the body switches
from upright, angular and thin

    into the hunched and leaning.

We change the walk –
from quick-step to a shamble

    and bargain on the change in silhouette.

We plus the years –
far easier than minus –

    we lose a height, we gain a weight, we settle

into an age we never hope to show.
It doesn't work. We do it all not knowing

    that what we imitate is what we are.

Like a pitchfork in a rick our age protrudes
and we are known, identified

to win the wave, the welcome –
the twenty minute small talk in the wind.

# Night Sweats

David makes a lame excuse
and limps away on his one good peg.

Amy, hunched as a question mark,
no longer listens, fails to hear.

Between the two lies a gawp, a chasm –
wide as a loch, as deep as sea.

But sometimes in a the night's hot sweat
he walks in, as bold as tuppence.

She stands up, as straight as maybe
and the two come close as the river's mercy,

safe as the anchor, the jetty, the quay:
proud as the masthead's fluttering flag.

# Bedtime Story

*to Minnie Mackenzie, aged 100*

In Minnie's laugh
the mouth is held

the perfect 'o', the fifteenth letter –
in brilliant, in sans serif.

There's nothing shifts
that Lilliput of symmetry –

its minuscule rotundity
a pearl, a pea, a pebble.

But in the reader's eye that 'o'
is majuscule, is upper case, is bold –

its fullface globularity
a sphere, an orb, a planet.

In each day's wakefulness, each sleep,
the mouth rings 'o', 'o', 'o' and 'o'.

Each dawn, in supposed contentment,
that o's a sun - its quick flame flickers.

But each night, in a seeming sadness,
that o's a moon – its spittle wanes.

Only the eyes firm terror questions
the true intent of the bedside reader.

Only the hollow wit confirms
the literal joke of the misread reading.

# Taking Leave

Lizzie is told that her departure
from the home she's known for forty years
is just a holiday. She is on leave.
She will like it where she's going.
It is not far. She will have fun.

She doesn't want to go. She makes it known
but that night her possessions are safe packed
in one old suitcase, in two black bin bags.
She finds a quiet threat in that neat stack
of her belongings left beside the bed.

If this was truly holiday she knows
they wouldn't pack as much of her as that.
Some things would certainly be left behind
to welcome her on her return. The moon
through the window casts light on the luggage.

There's something in black plastic seems to shift
a pulse of living light across the room.
She wants the curtains closed and grips the hand
which draws the rayon harshly on the rail.
That same metallic screech is in her cry.

Some person from some other bed shouts *'Stop!*
*Just let the others get to sleep!'*. She stops
but doesn't sleep. All night the thread of light
between the shutters drills in on the eye.
There is no morning known to her. No waking.

The trainee nurse who draws aside the curtain
across the March apology for sun
looks down on bed 6A, sees open eyes
fixed on the ceiling's central safety light.
Straight and to the point the old girl's gone.

And written in the book: *'No leave. No rehab.'*

44

# III

## Late Fire

The fire won't spit. It will only glow.
The lamp throws a shadow to the wall.
The whole of the world is this one room
where someone yawns. The clock's impatience
throws a loud voice to the round world's rim.

Somebody sleeps, a head grows heavy.
The unknown dream is disconnected
by that quick cut: to fact from fiction,
Somebody wakes and arises, shifts
the unknown world to the next known world.

# A Passionate Adventure

You live with this: the man, the woman
walking close to water. It is summer
but they are dressed as though approaching autumn.

He wears his climbing boots, his Levi's.
She wears her anorak. He holds her hand
and seems to coax the woman to be cautious,

to watch her step. Laughing, she lets go
and from the hand she quickly takes from his
he tugs a glove. She brags the wedding finger

and runs from him, daring him to chase
and so he does, right to the river's edge.
The floods of water muffle out the laughter.

Here the man, the woman, both collide
to child again. They simply dance on rock
all slippery with green weed from the water.

They must have known where they were going.
Perhaps it was to cross the stepping stones.
Perhaps it was the steep climb into woodland

where they knew leaf's shadowing would shield
their new embrace, desired discovery.
That journey was the passionate adventure

of one foot slipping, one hand reaching,
one hand gripping on to green but ripping
and then the sudden silence in rough water.

On the bank she left her anorak.
He left a skid, a boot mark on the rock.
Behind them stood the cottage with lace curtains

neatly drawn to keep the wedding cake.
Stacked upon the table were the presents.
For them there were no arguments, no favours.

You live with this: and on each recall
you hear the hammer thunder in the flood
and see the axe head in the river's silver.


*(i.m. Lynn and Barry Collett. Married, August 15th, 1998:
death by drowning, August 17th, 1998)*

# Safe Lupins

Those who outlive the winter muddle through.
The women, workers mellowed by their age,
return in city coats and scarves
to rake and hoe at earth which snow
had hardened into crust just hours ago.

Their husbands potter in the shed
or else are working, working still,
towards pensions or the statutory watch
in factories or offices.

There will be those who won't return,
who couldn't live to see the winter through.
Their plots begin to straggle until wives
come after them to tidy things away
or lock the gate the man left off the latch –
the last act banging with the wind.

A younger tenant follows from the list.
He lifts a spade and hacks at earth
which opens and recoils with root:
the first cut done, the quick hurt gone –
like trapping fingers in the door –
and something is possessed, made his.

The jobless seem to find some solace here
in labours more of love than cash.
They turn a hand far harder than they'd turn
for overlookers or the boss.
Their fitness ripples at the wrist
in wind too cool to raise a sweat.

Most winds are fair winds here, one's ill,
bearing the stench from factories.
I saw a man once, at his plot, turn green
at that stink from the selfsame place
he'd worked a life away to leave.

And still it got back to him, even here,
the south side of the river where
he's master of his twelve by twelve yard space,
hedged neatly off, protected from his friends.

Those neighbours from North Bank live streets away
and drive or cycle half a mile or more
for this small sanctuary they hold
from backyards and from living rooms
where smoke and soot is all that blooms.

Their plots are distant refuge from those wives
who fret and polish tidy homes
made fussy with cheap ornament.
No walls protect. We see far more
than neighbourly good manners should allow.

Gifts come to us. Come Spring the old house groans
with green and yellow burgeoning –
a promise of that future harvest when
our windows rattle with the seed
from those safe lupins which our neighbour grows
to screen us from his stately labouring.

## The Bullfinch & the Buffalo

'I met her quite by accident –
the good friend of a friend who went
to market in the market hall
the day I went. That's all, that's all.'

'There was some feint attraction when
I saw him stand among the men
that Friday afternoon. His style
was different, at least. That smile!'

All that was years and years ago
before both man and wife could know
how one harsh voice would say 'Goodnight',
and one hand clatter out the light.

## In Absentia

This morning, six-thirty,
the light of the sun
flickers through curtains
to brighten the room.

Two glasses, one empty the other half-full:
the dregs of *vin ordinaire* darkened and dull.

Wind in the willow tree
outside the window
throws a quick shadow
across the stone floor.

The corkscrew, still holding the prize of the night,
lies on the carpet: a stab in the sunlight.

Beside it the candle
has dribbled red wax
down from the bookshelf
on unopened mail.

On the bench, the broken bread, Caullomiers –
the poem, unfinished, crumpled on the chair.

## June 3

The first weak sun of summer
and the noises grow –
a mellowing of question into answer.

The heifer's bellow looms across the field,
the dog barks from the darkness of a barn,
the flies' persistent buzz strikes home
from distant air into the brain –
    in one ear it grinds through
    to the other.

But the most alien sound of all
the jets, which are grounded all harsh winter –
    that rage rips in one ear
    and sticks.

# Sir Pig

has lost his name.
That beast has lost all charm
to title. He won't work.
Last night the bitch's bark

was closer to each hoof
than ever dare. Just half
of her faked threat; each snip
played power but no snap

could quite out act the white
of her wall-eye. That weight
of pork had not a fear
for her conceit. No hair

on his back bristled; not
one cautious grunt, one snort
came out of him to warn
her off. He just got on

with apple for the gut.
Each apple he could get
well-satisfied each munch
of jowl and jaw. The stench

of cider on his breath
hung heavy as a broth
but nothing in him hung
where it was wanted. Long

we wanted him, and long
we waited, threatening
to take good apples back.
But nothing worked, no talk

could chat him up to act.
He just got on and knocked
the apples back. The sow
was brought to him. She saw

him chomping in the pen
and then she too began
to gob those apples which
had rattled from the hatch

of Gilpin's truck. No trick
could titillate the cock
in him. We tried the wand
of willow in the hand.

That did no good. He must
have felt it though. He pissed
all over apples, dripped
as he was walking: dropped

his waste on what was best
intended as a feast
to make him feel at home
and perk his sex. Not him.

He just got on with what
*he* wanted *when*. No shout
from us could interrupt
his diet. We just kept

enticing him with threat –
a warning that his throat
would slit. We kept him out
all night to serve him right.

No barking from the bitch
today. She saw what botch
I made in taking aim –
the eye, the hand, the arm –

and she was in there: teeth
sank as he fell. A truth
got home to her, the butt
cut to her back, the boot

sank in the rib. Her yap
was loud enough to rip
the sky - a yelp more harsh,
more bitter than the hush

in which he lay. In dim
of dawn's light he was dumb –
quite dumb. He took the shot
with just a huff. The shout

was mine. There was a kick
ran up the arm to knock
the clatter of that bolt
against that bone. We built

his gallows in god oak
and strung him high. No ache
came through the blade, that flash
of silver through the flesh

came easy but the spill
of blood was terrible.
We let him drip. That gash
I cut gave out a gush

of breath, a reek of sweet
where I had thought of sweat.
We left him on his tree
but at dusk went to try

to cut the belly out
and make the carcass light
to carry back by cart
in chop cuts. So we thought

but when that slit was made
we saw each apple slide
out of the weight he'd taken –
not one skin bruised, not broken.

# No Metamorphoses

Auden was awesome. The man's evasion disappointed.
He echoed Ovid: *'Our birth, our ancestry,*
*and that which we have not ourselves created,*

*can scarcely be called our own...'* but all the time
reaching, stretching forward, to tap the mike,
distort the sound: two fingers like a cloven hoof.

*'Next question!'* Oxford in the 20's, the influence
of Eliot? No word from Auden who swiftly palms
the question on to some apprentice underling.

All I hear is the wrong voice echo, all I see
the wrong lips sing. All I do is shuffle papers
wondering quite where can all this lead? *Try Sex?*

After the intended *'chat'*, a novice to a chosen master,
I head home disillusioned; by myself, my blunder
and by awkward Auden, with a hero's dumb rejection.

Nothing had changed. Still it was daylight, traffic
rumbled on. Some buses trundled, drivers
sounded horns. A white cloud drifted, easy in the sky.

It did not rain. I chose the nearest corner bar
and from dark mahogany raised a glass to Ovid
and to Auden: *'He himself teaches what I should do.*

*It is right to be taught by the enemy.'*

# No Moon, no Star

One year no light could pass into the room:
      no sun, no moon, no star.
Only the sound could tell the time, the weather:
the cockerel's crow, rain on the roof, the hammer.

Only the shadow darkening the window
could tell of someone walking past, not halting.
Only the quick, shock rattle of the latch –
      the message passed, the door left open
could tell of some event, some presence wanted.

      Across the window ivy thickened, clambered
      from pane to pane, across each jamb, each transom
      to block the light and filter; green.

      From inside, looking out, each growth
      gripped to the glass with clutching claws,
      hampered the eye and baulked the brain
      from all unwanted interruption.

No news was good, or so it seemed:
a world encased in shades of bottle green –
or aqua green or apple green –
depending on the mind, the mood, the body.

      But something interfered with calm:
      a single tip of finger entered
      between the frame and window head
      to beckon toward the darkness of the brain.

That shoot was pale and pallid but each root
      was parasitic, tumorous. Each whisker
      dithered deep in dark to find some grip
      or more rewarding anchorage.

It took some time to recognise the threat.
Each day seemed distant through the lattice leaf
of no world making no demands, no favours.
There was no spring, no summer but that winter
    came in the room with ice in ivy.

The scalpel bit into each stem, cut through
the bark and through each weave of root to free
the small room of its darknesses,
the dark brain of its mindless nothingness.

Each cut was easy, each snip snap
slit through the ivy's clamber over glass.
But when it came the time to try to tug
each rooted stem from its firm hold it held.

It would not free, not easily. It took
a chisel to chip through that wood to ease
the million witches' fingers from their grip.

    The job was done. A slow enlightenment.
    Inside the room was white, outside was white
    but each new crack, each crevice needed learning.

# Mirror, *Mirror*

Once he looked hopefully into the mirror
And wished his time onward into the mirror.

He wished himself inches, a moustache, a future –
A girl on his arm and a glint of the future.

What he foresaw was adventure, far distant –
A girl on his arm and a moustache, far distant.

He wished his time onward with god-speed and glory
But let the time pass in the mirror. His glory

Would halt all the calendars, diaries and clocks.
He could not halt minutes or seconds. The clocks

Kept ticking the time away, out of adventure.
He missed the right inches, right girl. No adventure

Made him aware of his glorious moment
Or taught him the moment that might be the moment.


## *Mirror*

For year after year he imagined the moment
Which lay far behind him. No mirror, no moment

Could bring back an image of unknown adventure.
He hopefully longed for a future adventure

When right on the minute, right second, the clocks
Would strike the right note and briefly the clocks

Would halt all the world in its footstep. That glory
Would hail the man in him a gallant, good glory.

Now that the minute is past and far distant
Minute is wrinkled on minute. Far distant

The girl on his arm has no glint of a future.
Not bloody, but bowed he looks into the future

And runs his time backwards out of the mirror
Each time he looks grievously into the glass.

## 'Warum, Warum...?'

Somewhere a choir
is singing Brahms –
'Warum ist das Licht gegeben?'.

The light of summer
flickers through the leaves;
on through the window
to the window ledge

where one last crane-fly
steps his final dance –
rising on a rising note
to hammer hammer at the lamp

then fall in perfect pirouette –
to entrechat and strike his tone
of counterpoint, discordancy.

His act, an angered arabesque,
a double shuffle heel-and-toe;
the wrong dance to the wrong motet –
'Warum ist das Licht gegeben?'.

Outside the window
light is beaming light;
from leaf to ivy and to earth –
all green on green upon a green.

Inside the head, the heart, the house
such light cannot be dimmed or dulled
by right or wrongful miserere.

The crane-fly wails
his whine of lachrymalis;
batters one leg from the other,
batters anger at the brain.

I turn him out
with his embittered song
to dance his danse macabre
and sing his sad song to himself –

*'Warum ist das Licht gegeben...?*
*Warum ist das Licht?'.*

# The Man who wrote 'Deutschland'

The man who wrote 'Deutschland'
completed his apprenticeship
    in numbers;

sometimes with napthol black
smudged into the needle's lesion
    in the skin.

In the beginning craft
was not his art; his numbers bruised
    and festered.

In seven years he passed
that master class which set the Jew
    from Gentile.

His cycle was complete –
his world turned from silence into
    insolence;

his art advanced to hearts
and daggers, eagles and adders –
    symbols and cyphers...

The boy unrolls his sleeve,
buttons his secret at the wrist
    and beneath the sleeve –

a plaster, snow-white lint;
beneath the lint, one word 'Deutschland'
    and a swastika.

IV

# Crab Apple

From yards away one tree outreaches grace
And strains each scraggy pincer-tip to sky.
That crab is weak. Each branch is out of place
And no leaf grows upon that sough and sigh
Where west winds whip each lateral to snap.
I want that tree a fist. I want a fight
Between the weather and the punch of sap –
The quick left hook, the upper cut, the right.

I take the ladder and the saw and climb
From earth to air among the leaf to find
My judgement suspect. Where to hack the rhyme
Of one branch with the other? I am blind
Inside the tree and have to clamber down
To judge each cut of adjective, each noun.

'Get thee Glass Eyes;
*and, like a scurvy politician, seem
to see things thou dost not.'*

KING LEAR Act IV, Scene VI

The politician and the poet
share initial p's
plus a little more despite
the poet's palinode of pleas
to contemplate the apposite
to be's, or not to be's.

To be the one p is to be
a grafter in the art
of making language glorify
the humphing of the heart
with verbiage and verity –
if not in toto, then in part.

The p of polished platitudes
will win acceptance late.
The youngster is the parvenu
who waits his age. Negate
the image of a rise in ruse
from rat to reprobate.

Negate the notion of the p –
the upstart; red or read –
who knows the bubble of repute.
In this life, lately lead,
the living win dubiety.
The most revered? The dead!

To be the one p leering in
to p's glass eye might gloat
on that reflection of the self

which is the truth. Connote
the mirror image *might* behind
the adverse opposition vote.

The poet and the politician
wring the change in view
from the good eye to the bad –
from left to right. Between the two
lies honesty, dishonesty –
the false reflects the true.

# Written on a Green Screen

*After Octavio Paz*

The green screen creates confusion:
an alphabet from which the letters blip,
words which foregather into sense or no sense,
sentences misconstrued as verses.

Let your words, O green one, be select, well chosen:
like the glare of neon on a New York hoarding,
like the first creation of the green zucchetto,
like the rustle of welcome in the greenback dollar.

Arse, armpit, nostril, ear,
eye socket fuddled by the umpteenth re-write,
the pupil distended as the stoned avocado,
eyelids that suffer the blinkered sunlight.

Your presence alarms an adjusted calm:
like the tv blue which sirens its closing.
You are rightly concerned by the poem's pinpricks:
examine the eye with its green acupuncture.

# From 'I': To 'I'
*for Stephen Spender (1909-1995)*


To put the pen to paper links the two:
the writer and the reader realign
from one 'I' to the other 'I', to 'You'.

No longer need the reader wonder who
the writer is. The two 'I's intertwine:
to put the pen to paper links the two.

The single aim of one first person's view
might claim the language back, from me to mine –
from one 'I' to the other 'I', to 'You'.

So is it that each 'I' provides a clue
to what 'I write', 'I read', between each line.
To put the pen to paper links the two

who hopefully will never misconstrue
the central 'I's subservient decline:
from one 'I' to the other 'I', to 'You'.

The first 'I' is the writer's I.O.U.
to those who 'They' first read. In grand design
'We' put the pen to paper, link the two
from one 'I' to the other 'I'. *'To You!'*

## 'Returns of the Day'

Always in the mind's eye is the picture
Of some event thought worthy of recall –
Some incident, some accident, some moment
When one split second froze home on the eye.

    It's never right, not quite. In that quick click
    From present into past the future fixes
    The fantasy of fiction onto fact –
    Right face, right smile, a wrong light
        Through the window.

Year after year that picture will return
From how things were to how they could have been –
Or how they should have been to how they were.
And so the double image is created –

    The one more right than wrong; the other, wrong!
    Year after year the two are readjusted
    Until both fact and fantasy collide –
    Wrong face, wrong smile, the right light
        Through the window.

But in each readjustment what is wanted
Is something which secures the mood, the meaning,
Of each return, each other close to other –
The two not a hundred miles apart.

# Afterthought

I wouldn't want the passer-by to care
what kind of leaf it is, what kind of tree,
what kind of fruit each knotted bough will bear.
I wouldn't want the saw to guarantee
the work of man was recognised. Each scar
should pass unnoticed, hidden underneath
the eye's acceptance of the foliar
where winds weave leaf and blossom into wreath.

I wouldn't want the shape I make to show
the muscle of the work, the way I cut
each leader to its height. The touch and go
of what to prune, and when, was painful but
all that is best forgotten by those made
to judge the makar's labour with the blade.

*Photo: Simon Thackray*

PETE MORGAN's first full-length collection of poetry appeared from Secker & Warburg in 1973. In 1976 he was one of a team of six British poets invited to tour the United States as part of the American Bicentennial celebrations. He has also visited France and Spain under the auspices of the British Council. He has held a number of creative writing appointments, notably Arts Council Fellow in Poetry at the University of Loughborough. Two further full-length collections have appeared from Secker and one from Ceolfrith Press. Pete Morgan currently lives in the East Yorkshire market town of Beverley.

Recent publications in
Arc Publications' series
POETRY FROM THE UK / IRELAND
edited by Jo Shapcott
include:


LIZ ALMOND
*The Shut Drawer*

JONATHAN ASSER
*Outside The All Stars*

DONALD ATKINSON
*In Waterlight: Poems New, Selected & Revised*

THOMAS A CLARK
*The Path to the Sea*

TONY CURTIS
*What Darkness Covers*

JULIA DARLING
*Sudden Collapses in Public Places*
*Apology for Absence*

CHRISSIE GITTINS
*Armature*

MICHAEL HASLAM
*The Music Laid Her Songs in Language*
*A Sinner Saved by Grace*

JOEL LANE
*Trouble in the Heartland*

HERBERT LOMAS
*The Vale of Todmorden*

IAN POPLE
*An Occasional Lean-to*

SUBHADASSI
*peeled*

MICHELENE WANDOR
*Musica Translapina*

JACKIE WILLS
*Fever Tree*